Can't You See Me Scream?

Discovering the Silence of Child Sexual Abuse

G.C. Peyton

Can't You See Me Scream;
Discovering the Silence of Child Sexual Abuse

Copyright © January 2014 By G.C. Peyton

Edited by Stephanie Montgomery
Unique Communications Concepts

Cover Design by Family First Designs

ISBN 978-0-9831637-9-4
Printed In the United States of America
First Edition Printing
January 2014

ChosenButterfly Publishing
P.O Box 515
Millville, NJ 08332
www.cb-publishing.com

Dedication.....

This book is dedicated to all the children and their families whose lives have been forever changed by sexual abuse. May they receive God's merciful healing and experience the freedom of forgiveness to grow and live beyond their pain.

To those who act fearlessly to break the silence of sexual abuse--may the wings of angels continue to lift you up and soar you above any obstacles in your way. May you always remember that God has not given us a spirit of fear; but of power, and of love, and of a sound mind to accomplish all that He has for us to do.

Table of Contents

Preface.....

The greatest miracle in the world to me is giving birth. To see your baby for the first time is an experience that some cannot put into words; even though you know it's the greatest joy you've ever felt. You're all prepared: you've got the bottles, diapers, blankets, baby furniture and all the neat little clothes. Finally, after all the months of waiting, the magical moment is here. You look into your baby's eyes and your heart melts. You are now a parent with a huge responsibility. So, off to home you go. But wait - they didn't give us the manual. So, what do we do now? If you're like most of us, you learn as you go.

There is no manual for raising kids that will guarantee what your experience will be or how they will turn out. You do your best and pray for the same. I always thought that when I had children, they would be like me. They would sit quietly and do what they are told... da-da, da-da, da-da (well, not exactly). One of my biggest 'ah-ha' moments as a parent was when I discovered that children are people too. They have their own personalities and they do things the way they are wired to. Even with that realization, we are still challenged repeatedly with being a parent and raising kids. We don't always know what to do in every situation; we don't always have the right answer and we don't always make the right decisions - but we try our best. Sometimes we miss the mark and don't interpret the signs correctly. Sometimes it's a minor thing that doesn't matter much, however sometimes it's huge and we miss the signs completely. Sometimes it's because we close our eyes and ears; however, sometimes our eyes and ears are wide open but the deafening silence prevents us *from seeing and hearing. When our eyes and ears are wide open, there can be other factors and forces preventing us from seeing through the veil and hearing the screams. Child sexual abuse is one of those ugly nightmares where unfortunately, we sometimes miss the signs and don't hear or see the screams. This is the story of silent screams.*

Chapter 1

Introduction to a Nightmare

Through the eyes of a child, I could say that I grew up with rose-colored glasses. We had a typical family for the time; dad worked and mom was a housewife. We certainly didn't have everything we wanted, but we surely had everything we needed. Life was good.

I was born and raised in one of the big cities in America by two, loving parents. I am the middle child between an older sister, a brother and a younger sister. To say I had the 'middle child' syndrome would be putting it mildly. Everyone seemed to have something special about them. My older sister wore the tag as the oldest. My brother wore the tag as the only boy. My younger sister wore the tag of being the baby. Hmmm, what did I have that was special about me? Well, I eventually learned that my parents were happy when we did well in school, so I began to wear that as my tag - 'good in school'. I wanted to make them happy. I am the only one in my family who graduated from college, then continued my educational goals to earn post-graduate degrees. I love my family and I love God. Life is good.

Growing up, my life was wonderful. Our parents clearly loved each other, they loved us - and they showed it. I can remember seeing our mom and dad dancing together as us kids sat on the couch and giggled. Our giggling soon turned to dread when mom and dad would reach out for us to join in the dancing. Oh no, here we go again! Trust me, we were more than happy being spectators. Daddy often told us how much he loved our mother and she returned that love by how she took care of him and us. Daddy was really strict; Mommy was more lenient and she often comforted us after we were disciplined. I think giving out punishments hurt Daddy more than it hurt us, but he knew what needed to be done if they wanted their kids to grow up right. I quickly learned from watching my older sister and brother get in trouble that I didn't want to be on the receiving end of that discipline. I often was the lone holdout when they were deciding to carry out one scheme or another. It didn't make me very popular when they got in trouble and I didn't. Ah... another tag to wear - 'miss goody two-shoes'. This tag was certainly not chosen by me. I carried those two tags throughout my life. I love education and I try to do well, being the best person I can be. I don't always get it right, but my heart is always trying.

Now as the mother of 2 adult daughters, much of what I learned growing up continues to kick in, even though they are no longer children. Parenting doesn't stop just because your kids grow up. My daughters have very different personalities. My youngest - Tara, is practical, hard-working and has a gentle personality, but can be a bit of a shark when she needs to. You could even say she is rough around the edges at times. I've had a lot of practice at holding my breath with her, wondering what was coming next. Growing up, she was the one we knew could handle any situation. In school, she was always fighting the fight for herself and anyone else - always willing to make a point of what's right and fair. One instance I recall is when another student wasn't wearing uniforms to school. Tara couldn't understand why that student could do this and she couldn't. Needless to say, she hated wearing uniforms. I told her that maybe the student's parents didn't have the money to buy uniforms. She quickly pointed out that the student was wearing Timberland boots and if they could buy those, they could buy uniforms. Thinking quickly, I said, "Maybe someone gave them the boots." She remorsefully - yet reluctantly, acknowledged that this could be true and she stepped down from that soapbox.

God loves variety and he surely didn't hold back when he gave me kids. My oldest daughter - Bria, is quite the opposite of her younger sister. While her personality can be described as calm and meek - she can be explosive at times. She has a fiery side to her that won't back down from a fight. There was an incident when she was in high school where a girl who didn't like her, decided that she was going to fight Bria. As Bria exited her classroom she was met with a punch to the side of her face. A fight ensued, parents were called and the girls were suspended from school. Bria's dad picked her up from school and we discussed the incident when they got home. Seeing the blood on her blouse, her dad asked where she was bleeding from. Bria quickly said, "That's her blood, not mine." Dad couldn't help letting a smile come across his face when he realized that she had held her own.

My life is good, but like everyone else - there are challenges and family issues that arise occasionally. Like most, I deal with family issues or 'bumps in the road' when they occur and I move on. This year however, I encountered a family issue that wasn't just a 'bump in the road' – it was an earthquake that would shake and rattle my world into pieces. A visit from my younger sister was all it took to change my life and my entire foundation forever.

My younger sister and I had not seen or talked to each other for almost a decade. The reason for our estrangement varies depending on who you ask; I thought it was for one reason, she later told me it was something else. In the end, it really was the same reason; we just looked at it differently from our own perspectives. Despite our differences, it didn't matter - she is my sister, I love her and was glad she had come to visit. She and her husband had come to visit my mother and we spent time together every day that weekend. The first day, we spent time alone sitting on our mother's bed holding hands and talking about old times. It felt just like we were kids again sitting on our own beds in the house we grew up in. It seemed like time had stood still.

On the last day of her visit, I got up early to spend time with her before she headed back home. It was during that time she told me something that had burdened her and impacted her life for years. She wanted to get it off her chest and I was all ears - but I wasn't prepared for what she was about to reveal. As I sat anticipating what she would say, I had a sinking feeling in my stomach. This must be serious. Was she dying? Was she and her husband having problems? Was something wrong with her kids? All that paled in comparison to what came next. She told me that she had been sexually-abused as a child. My shock was written all over my face. The tears came and I froze, not knowing what to do. I listened and quietly cried. The pain was intense, but not as bad as it would get. The pain deepened when she revealed her abuser - our brother.

My younger sister began sharing details of the excruciating pain she endured by carrying this secret around for more than 20 years. She had not remembered the abuse until she was an adult. At that time, she was involved in a case in which one of the children in her day care was being abused and my sister had to testify at the trial. Suppressed memories had spared her from remembering her own abuse during her childhood, but it had surely had an impact on her adult life. Memories haunted her and she decided the only way she could move forward - and hopefully beyond it, was to address and release the pain of her past. My mind was racing. How did I miss this growing up? How did any of us not see what was happening in our home? Did we unwittingly ignore the signs - or was our brother so manipulative, he knew exactly when to strike and remain under the radar? A million questions swirled in my mind without answers. During a phone call to my brother, my younger sister actually confronted him about her memories. Surprisingly, he admitted to abusing her. During their hours-long conversation, two questions he would not answer; why he stopped and what he did or said to make her not tell anyone. My younger sister was always the 'tattle tale' of our family - if you wanted anything to remain secret, you kept it away from her. The fact that she never said anything at the time to my older sister or me, or our parents - only added more questions to the list growing in my head.

Our brother separated himself from our family unit years ago. He was different from my siblings and I - but as time went on we didn't question it. We all had our theories and they amounted to one thing - he was just weird. He was who he was and we were who we were; case closed. It's amazing how children can be raised in the same house, with the same parents - yet become very different people. Well, I did say that God loves variety! Our brother seemed to become distant when he was about 12 years old. Up until that time, we played like most siblings and had the same friends in the neighborhood. At the time he began to change, it didn't seem so odd because we thought he was 'coming into his own' since he was becoming a teenager. After all, he was the only boy, so what did we know? We thought 'that's what boys do'. He began spending time by himself in his room. He started listening to music that was different from what we had known growing up. He liked music from artists such as Three Dog Night, Led Zeplin and Blood, Sweat & Tears. Different - but everybody is entitled to what they like. Again, there goes God's variety!

No matter how many times I try to wrap my mind around the insanity I have been told, I can't grasp it. My mind refuses to accept the unthinkable. I have so many chaotic and disturbing thoughts running through my brain; so many questions without answers. What are you supposed to do when you discover information that is so vile and devastating to a family unit? I don't believe there is a clear answer to such a question; however, I knew I had to do one thing for sure - support my sister and be there for her, no matter what. My sister needed to vent and to release this beast of a burden and she also needed my support. I assured her that I would be there for her no matter what she needed, no matter what time of the day or night. All she needed to do was call.

My sister told me that after she confronted our brother years ago, she then confronted our mother. Addressing this matter with our mother was a futile act. Could it be perhaps she too, had repressed memories of knowing what her son had done to one of her precious daughters? Surely a mother knows her child, his or her temperament and habits - both good and bad? Maybe acknowledging them is something more difficult to admit? More thoughts, more questions. I found it interesting that although my mother did not admit knowing what occurred years ago, she certainly did not deny it *could have* happened. I heard very clearly what my sister said my mother told her - as well as what my mother *did not* say during their discussion that day. She selectively chose the words; "You never told me", not the words 'I didn't know'. On some level, this was not a complete surprise. Our mother always seemed to 'protect' our brother - or maybe it was more like 'baby' him. Our father even mentioned this on occasion. Our father was a man's man with a strong ego, but in a good way. He was certainly what a strong father should be and he wanted his son to be the same. Mom surely loved us all; however, I think she carried a little something extra for our brother because he was the only boy. I don't know this to be a fact, but maybe she thought dad put too much pressure on my brother as he strived to raise him to be a man? Perhaps she compensated for the pressure in other ways. However it was meant to be, it presented itself as babying him.

I'm sure our mom meant well. I always looked up to her as a great mother, not only to us - but to many people who were part of our life growing up. She was - and still is, 'Mom' to a lot of people; but sometimes even the best of intentions from the best people are wrought with unintended results. I am certainly not saying that our mother's treatment of our brother caused him to abuse, but I do have many questions and doubts about what she knew and when.

Chapter 2

Can't Wake Up Yet- The Nightmare is Not Over

My brother molested my sister when she was very young: my brother molested my sister…my brother…my sister…molestation… this must be a dream.

In my discovery that the life I thought was so idyllic - was in fact tinged with a nightmarish secret, I can't help but feel numb with disbelief. In the midst of attempting to process this discovery of sexual abuse by talking to my sister, the magnitude of my nightmare became even more real. Not only did my brother molest my younger sister for 3 years beginning when she was 3 years old - he also attempted to molest my oldest sister's middle daughter when she was 10! My brother would have been 28 at the time, by the way. So, this was no longer a child abusing another child; this was an adult attempting to abuse a child. "This can't be", I tell myself. Not in our family. We were so 'normal'. Oddly enough, I would discover that my younger sister told my oldest sister about her abuse at the same time she told our mother. To our knowledge however, my older sister chose not to confront my brother as my younger sister had. How could she not discuss this? This was surely not her character. She could be a 'bull in a china shop' when she wanted to. If she wanted to shake your world, she would. Her response (or lack of it) made no sense to me, but I didn't want to spend time on that at the moment. I chose to think that maybe my niece begged her not to do anything; nothing happened, so just leave it alone. I accepted that for the time being.

As the nightmare continues to unfold, I discover that more than two decades of family secrets have resulted in a growing list of casualties, including my younger sister and my niece. Mind you, these were the ones that we knew about. I couldn't help but wonder how many more there might have been. People have always said that crisis will bring out a person's true character and nature. During the tough times, if you watch and listen carefully to those around you - undoubtedly you will find out what you need to know about them. It is also said that if you go digging and searching for something, you will eventually find something you might not like. How true both of these adages were, as the following year would reveal.

After my younger sister and I reconnected, we pledged to keep in contact often. During that year, my sister and I talked on a number of occasions about the impact her abuse had on her life. We often talked and cried. I was glad I was able to be there for her and share this burden. However, at one point during that year, several weeks went by and I did not hear anything from her. She was not responding to my text messages or phone calls. After a while, I didn't want to keep bugging her, so I reluctantly accepted that maybe life had gotten in the way and she was busy and didn't have time. Even though I was disappointed, I surely could understand that. Finally, one day she called out of the blue. I had prayed that she would.

I was glad to hear from her and told her so. Even in the midst of my excitement to finally talk to her, I quickly sensed that this was more than just a call to say 'Hi' and chat. As I would soon discover, that conversation would expose more secrets. Another casualty is revealed. My sister confided in me that *my* oldest daughter Bria, had also been abused by our brother. Bria had confided in my sister, but begged her not to tell me or anyone. She said that no one could know, so my sister reluctantly agreed to stay silent. She knew the feeling; after all, she had walked in her shoes herself. However, time would reveal that my sister could not keep this to herself, so she called me. Well, if I was saddened and shocked at the news that my sister was abused - just imagine how I felt now hearing that my daughter, *my* precious baby, was also abused. I had fire in my eyes, hatred in my heart and pain in the pit of my stomach. I knew Bria didn't want me to know this and she had sworn my sister to secrecy, but how could I hold this inside? For me, it wasn't a matter of 'if' I would blow the lid on this, but how and when.

My most pressing thought at that moment was that my daughter has been hurt - is still hurting and I needed to soothe her pain. Nothing else mattered or was more important at the time, however I knew that timing and approach was all too important. There was a trust factor that I needed to seriously consider and I wanted to do this with minimal additional pain and casualty. After further discussion with my sister, we felt it might do more harm than good for me to confront my daughter with this revelation at that particular time. She was going through some issues of her own, so the timing of our discussion was most important. So for about a month; as hard as it was, I bore this secret in silence, waiting for the right moment to act. Then one night, our phone rang at 2:30 a.m. My husband - who usually sleeps through everything, woke up immediately. It was my sister. She was having 'an episode'. Something had triggered memories of her abuse and she couldn't sleep. The strange thing was that I had also been awake for a while because I couldn't sleep, so her call gave me something to do. I would have welcomed a more pleasant call though.

Again, we talked and cried; talked and cried. After a couple hours of talking and feeling her pain immensely, my soul told me that I could no longer keep the secret about my daughter. I broke the news to my sister and told her I must talk to my daughter. To my surprise, she was relieved and said that she was glad I was going to do it and that she didn't mind if I told Bria that she was the one who told me. I certainly respected the position of confidence she was put in, so I decided that I wouldn't reveal my source initially; but I was sure my daughter would figure it out quickly. 'I'll cross that bridge when I come to it', I thought. I've got deeper water to tread right now.

What is my game plan? Who do I confront first? How do I approach this? I think I'll pray; *God, how I need you now!* My mind clears quickly; I have work to do. First, I must talk to my mother. I figured that I could approach her in a couple of different ways; one from the standpoint of her knowing about my sister's abuse and never telling me - and the other would be to give her a heads-up that her son may be going to jail. Not much of a choice, but what else have I got to work with? I didn't write the script and I surely didn't select the players. I decided that I was going to talk to her on Saturday morning, which was just a couple days away. I spent much of the night before tossing and turning in bed - finally waking up some time around 2:00 a.m. and pondering my thoughts until about 4:00 a.m. I woke my husband and told him what had occurred, but I sensed he had known there was something going on. After talking for about 2 hours, he asked if I was sure I wanted to confront my mother. He was concerned about what it might do to her. I told him I was sure our relationship was strong enough to withstand the much-needed and unavoidable conversation. As I got dressed and prepared for the drive ahead, how I prayed that I was right.

The hour drive to my mother's house was long; seemingly much longer than usual. I was in a hurry, but also wanted to drive slowly in order to sort out my thoughts and prolong the inevitable. I knew this would be such a critical conversation and I surely didn't want to blow it. I had prepared myself for the possibility that my mother may again go into 'denial mode'; as she had done with my younger sister when she confronted our mother about the abuse she suffered. I prayed I would be able to handle it and stay calm if she did. I told my mother I was coming and that I needed to talk to her. I did not give her any indication about what I wanted. As I was driving, I was thinking about my mother. She didn't know what I wanted to talk about, so I was wondering what her thoughts were as she waited for me to arrive; *Am I sick? Are my kids ok? Are my husband and I ok? Did something tragic happen?* I couldn't help but think how she would feel when I ultimately told her. As I usually do, I called her when I was about 10 minutes away. I think I sensed a change in her voice. When I got to her home, I didn't waste any time getting to the point.

I sat down and I told my mother everything that I had discovered about my brother abusing my daughter. I also told her I knew about my younger sister. The tears and the anger welled up in me again. *My brother molested my daughter...how could he do this - again?* The reaction in my mother's response was similar to what it had been when my sister called her. I believe her first word was a feigned 'What?' spoken in a surprised sort of tone. I tried hard to stay as calm as I could, keeping the focus on informing her and not interrogating her. I continued to tell her what I knew about both my sister's and my daughter's abuse. I told her that I wanted to kill him (Ah... now here comes a more expressive reaction from her). She reaches over to put her arm on my shoulder and tells me that I really didn't want to do that. So I think, '*Okay, are you concerned about me or him*'? I make it clear to her that I 'feel' like killing him, but I am smart enough to know that I don't want to spend the rest of my life in jail - and surely not because of him. I talked a bit more about the situation, but I was amazed that she really didn't ask me many questions. I was surprised, but not surprised. After all, she didn't react much when my sister told her she had been abused.

I told my mother I wanted to talk to my brother. I hadn't seen or talked to him in over 10 years, so I didn't have any contact information for him. I asked for his phone number. She gave it to me, but I am not sure if she really wanted to. I then asked where he lived and she asked if I was going over there. She said that if I wanted to go there, she would go with me. I was not ready to talk to him yet and I surely didn't want her to be there when I did. I had more conversations to have before I talked to him. I was thinking about the conversations I needed to have and it occurred to me that I needed to talk to my youngest daughter. I found out about my oldest daughter, but I didn't know if anything had happened to my *youngest* daughter. I got the immediate feeling that I needed to go to her. I told my mother I had to go and she asked if I thought my brother had done anything to my youngest daughter. I angrily told her that I didn't know. At that point, anything could have happened.

I gathered my belongings and prepared to leave when my mother asked if it was something that she did that could have made him do the things he was accused of. She then asked how she could have given birth to someone who could do such things. She also asked if I blamed her. I told her I didn't know how I felt right then. I didn't think I blamed her, but if she knew this was going on - then my feelings might be different. My head was spinning - I had to go. I couldn't listen to her self-imposed pity party. This was not about her. It was about my daughter! I respect my mother, but right then - this was not about her. I couldn't listen to her chatter. I didn't care how she felt. I cared about stopping the hurt in my daughter. I got up to go and when I got to the door, my mother began to cry. She said that she was sorry, but I'm not sure about what. Was she sorry that it happened? Was she sorry that she never told me? What did she mean? I couldn't bear to ask at that moment. I had to go. I put on my sunglasses to mask my tears as I walked down the hall to the elevator. I got to the lobby and thought about how the crystal chandeliers and the courteous doorman that I usually marvel at, now seemed oblivious to me behind my tears. I called my youngest daughter when I got to my car. I told her that I needed to talk to her right away and it had to be in person. She said she was home and would wait for me to get there. What more would I find out? How would I handle it if I discovered that she too had been abused? I didn't believe I could handle it if she too had been abused. I prayed, *God, please don't let this nightmare deepen.*

Here we go again, another long ride ahead. This time, I was in a hurry. I had to get there quickly. I had to know now! I arrived at my daughter's home, sat down and told her the importance of my visit. I began to tell her about her sister being abused and told her I needed to know if anything inappropriate had ever happened to her. Thank God she said it hadn't. I asked if it were possible that she just couldn't remember. She assured me that she only remembers being around my brother once - maybe twice and it was always when a lot of people were around. Thank God for guardian angels!

We talked about what this all meant. She said that maybe the revelation of all this will help her sister overcome some challenges that have plagued her for some time. My daughters are no exception to sibling rivalry. They love each other, but certainly have had their share of sibling moments. So, hearing my younger daughter acknowledge that the abuse probably impacted her sister, touches my heart and brings a measure of comfort in the midst of this turmoil. We certainly needed to support each other at a time like this. After more conversation, I went home. My mind is bursting with all sorts of thoughts. What's my next move? It's time to talk to my oldest daughter Bria. I didn't look forward to having any of these conversations, but I really didn't want to have this one. I knew this was real, but talking to Bria would bring the reality home in a way that I wasn't sure I was ready to experience. What would she say? Would she admit it? Would she say that she didn't want to talk about it, as my younger sister had warned? Would she be angry that I found out? All these thoughts flooded my head and I just wanted to crawl in bed and escape to a much-needed sleep, but I knew I had come too far to stop now. I got home and gave my husband an update on the day's events. His comforting voice and assurance that he felt my pain were a welcoming, guilty pleasure. How could I feel pleasure at a time like this? God put him in my life for a reason and he certainly was fulfilling his purpose right at that time.

After talking to my husband, I called Bria to tell her I needed to talk to her as soon as possible. She began to ask what was wrong. "Did I do something? Am I in trouble?" Amazing how your kids always will be kids. Even as an adult and a mother herself, she still reacts to that all-too-familiar parental voice of alarm. I told her that we needed to talk face to face. She said she would be over soon. I sat there again feeling like I was in a barrel quickly going over Niagara Falls.

Chapter 3

The Backstory – The Why Behind the What

Every story has a backstory. I've heard it said that for every situation, there is a 'why' to every 'what'. Never can we just look at someone and know exactly who they are and why they act as they do, without knowing where they've been or how they got there.

Over the years, my relationship at times with my oldest daughter has been somewhat complicated. I can't even say that I really understand it completely. One day we are warm and loving, having a great time; the next day we are at odds over something that one of us thinks is trivial and the other thinks is a major earthquake. I love her as deeply as any mother could love her child and I am sure that she loves me, but we definitely are the poster children for 'oil and water'; you can mix them up, but eventually they will separate. It disheartens me that we go through this and I have tried many, many times to help us find solutions to avoid this roller- coaster relationship - but sadly, I have not been successful. Let me tell you however, I don't see this as 'doom and gloom'; we just view some things very differently and we both are passionate about our own points of view. Here goes God's variety at work again!

Bria has had her share of challenges in life. She has made some poor choices and I can honestly say that I haven't completely understood them all. The discovery that she has been abused is giving me a bit of clarity and understanding for some of it. Bria's father and I broke up when she was two years old and I am sure it affected her in several ways. Of course she would no longer see him on a daily basis, but she would also have to experience the disappointment of him not showing up when he was supposed get her. Any mother who has been in this situation knows the pain of seeing your child stand at the window and wait for their father. In your heart, you know that he is more than likely not going to show up. You don't want to jump the gun and do anything about it yet, because you are also quietly hoping that he does. You also know that when he doesn't show, you are left to deal with the aftermath. You must pick up the pieces of their hurt and disappointment, which usually manifests itself in their behavior for days to come.

A few years after Bria's father and I broke up - I married, so Bria had a step-father come into her life. The next year, she had a baby sister. Bria was a great big sister; often jumping up and trying to tend to whatever her sister's need was at the time. When Bria went to middle school, we started to see a change in her behavior. I know that this is often a time of change for kids, so we attributed much of it to the normal growth process. Her school work was being impacted, so we naturally became more concerned. Bria was always the type of student who had to work hard for every grade. School did not come easy for her. Her step-father and I had been involved parents; we always went to school for the typical open houses, meetings, random 'pop' visits and especially upon request when there was a problem. As this continued to be a challenge, we concluded that she was going through the typical pre-teen syndrome; however, we wanted to be sure. We decided to seek counseling. We wanted to make sure that any help she needed, she had. We definitely did not want years to go by and then find out that there was something that we had missed that could have been resolved years earlier.

Once we decided to get help, I recall talking to the counselor and telling her that I was open to finding out anything that might be causing Bria to have problems - even abuse. I had no reason to think that she had been abused, but I wanted to cover all the bases. We didn't let the girls go over anyone's house unless the mother was home; we certainly felt our home was safe, but I wanted every stone unturned as we tried to understand her behavior. The counselor eventually assured me they felt that Bria had not been abused. Bria had denied it and they had found nothing to indicate otherwise. I was relieved. At least - I thought, we can cross this off the list. Little did I know that she was skillfully covering up the truth and the years to come would reveal her silent pain.

As I sat and waited for my daughter to arrive, I was filled with many different emotions. Over the last several days; I felt anger, rage, hurt, sorrow and believe it or not - relief. Now the feeling of relief might sound strange to some, but to me it was a sweet relief. This feeling of sweet relief comes from finally knowing that there is something tangible that has been triggering my daughter's behavior and choices all these years. It may not be the total cause, but abuse is such an incredibly-huge issue, that it can have devastating impacts which span across a person's life and the lives of those around them. At least now I had a place to start in sorting things out with her. I quietly asked God to guide and direct me as I talked with her. I knew that He had not brought me this far to leave me now.

Bria arrived and I was so glad to see her. Not only because we needed to talk, but because she had been a bit distant with me for the past week. I wasn't really sure about what - but that's nothing unusual, so I just decided to let it play out. During those times when we are at odds, my wish is always that time will close the hole in whatever link has been opened. This time was no different, but the magnet that drew us back together this time was something that no one would have wished for.

I asked Bria to come upstairs to my room so we could talk. We sat on the bed. I glanced up and noticed the look on her face. It was a look of anticipation and uncertainty. Knowing what I knew - I wanted to reach out , hug her and just cry; but I really needed to hold myself together if I was going to get through this. I decided to cut to the chase. I told Bria I just found out some important information and I needed to ask her some questions. I informed her that I had already talked to her sister. I told her that I would understand if she didn't want to answer or talk about the issue, but I was desperately praying that she would. I asked her if anyone has ever done anything inappropriate to her. Without hesitation she looked at me and said, "Yes". My heart sank and the tears began to fall.

I could feel the breath leave my chest and my throat felt as if someone was trying to shove a tennis ball down it. I felt like I couldn't move, but I managed to ask her who it was and she said that it was my brother. I lowered my head and cried. The pain got worse - I didn't think it could. Even though I knew this information, the reality of hearing it directly from my daughter brought about a pain that I couldn't have prepared myself for. How could a mother ever prepare herself for such unspeakable pain caused by such an unspeakable act committed against her child? I sat there saying over and over how I felt like killing him. I grasped for the words to ask the right questions to get more details, but I was uncertain about how to go about it. I didn't want to make her uncomfortable or pressure her to talk about something she was probably ashamed and embarrassed about, but I had to keep going.

Child sexual abuse victims often feel like the abuse is their fault; however, it is *never, ever* their fault. The feeling of shame and embarrassment is natural. Their abusers know how to ensure that. Almost as if on cue to rescue me from my stalled state, Bria began to talk about the abuse that occurred. She told me it happened when she would go to my mother's house while I was going to school in the evening. At that time, I wanted to finish my degree so my mother would pick Bria up from school and take her to her house while I was in class. I can't recall if I was in class one or two nights a week. I would get Bria after class and we would go home. I thought she was safe - I didn't have any reason to think otherwise. After all, she was with Grandmom!

My brother lived not far from my mother's house, so he would go there occasionally. His visits would sometimes occur when Bria was there. When my younger sister revealed that Bria confided this to her, I feverishly struggled to figure out the timeframe. Bria just confirmed what I had concluded. Bria's abuse had taken place between the time periods when she was four years old, until shortly after she turned five. It didn't help much, but it was at least some measure of consolation that the time period had not been longer. Make no mistake about it - a second of abuse is too long. Bria's dad and I had broken up by this time and he was not dependable. When I decided to go back to school, my mother enthusiastically offered to help with Bria. I saw this as a welcome resolution to my issue of where Bria would be while I was in school. My mother had always jumped at the opportunity to watch her grandchildren. These times would be either while we worked when daycare was closed - or if we were just going out for a while or simply for overnight visits. Having Bria go there while I was in school was welcoming and since my dad had passed away the year before, it also gave my mother company. I had about a year to go before I would finish school, so this was a perfect fit.

Shear horror welled up in me more and more as we talked. This was the realization I was afraid of. I needed to know more - however, I didn't really want to know details. I also knew I had to find out what happened. I will spare the horrible details and only share less-intrusive aspects. Bria revealed how my brother would wait until my mother went upstairs. It was during these times when my brother would abuse Bria. As Bria continued talking, I felt like I was not breathing. I think I was unconsciously holding my breath in anticipation of the next horrible detail. I knew all too well which detail I definitely did not want to hear - penetration. I didn't want to hear it, but I knew I had to ask the extent of the abuse. How would I do this? I decided to gently ask what he had done to her. She confirmed that there was no act of penetration. At the time, I wasn't sure if she was withholding this detail or if it was accurate. I would soon receive confirmation in the days to come.

We spent more time talking. I wanted to ask her why she never told me, but I also didn't want her to think this was her fault in any way. Sometimes asking that question makes victims think because they didn't tell anyone - it's their fault. Thankfully, Bria continued to talk and eventually said that my brother told her that if she told anyone what was happening, then she would be taken away. My heart breaks some more. I think about how she lost her father because our relationship had ended and now she was being made to fear she may also lose her mother. What choice did she have but to stay silent?

I am heartbroken, but through my tears I told her how sorry I was that this happened to her. I talked about my younger sister and the difficult time she has encountered in dealing with her abuse. I was feeling the deepest hurt that a mother could possibly feel right then. Someone has hurt my child and I wasn't there to do anything about it. I spent a lot of time thinking about the 'what ifs'. What if I had not gone to school? What if I had stayed with her father? What if I had someone else watch her instead of having her go to my mother's house? What if she had told me? What if I had been able to see the signs of abuse? What if... What if... What if? I tried to reason with myself that I had no way of knowing my child would be abused. I certainly didn't see any signs and I had no reason to believe my daughter would not be safe at her grandmother's house. Had I known, she would never have been there. I also tried to tell myself that the decisions that I made - in and of themselves, were good ones. For example, if I had stayed with her father it would have meant having me and my child in a destructive and dangerous environment. Not finishing college, might have possibly meant I would not have been able to support us properly. Some answers I know for sure; others are 'maybes'. We continued to talk and I asked her how she was feeling. She said that she had put the abuse out of her mind and doesn't think about it. I know on some level this is probably true; however I also know that it has and still, impacts her life now.

As we talked about what to do, I told Bria I was going to confront my brother. I had to - I needed to, I must. Bria said she was okay with that, but she didn't want to see or talk to him. I respected that and didn't pressure her to do otherwise. I also asked if she was okay with me talking to my older sister and my nieces. She said she was fine with that also. I explained to her that I intended to get to the bottom of things to break the silence and to stop the cycle of abuse and its aftermath as best I could. Although it has been years since the abuse happened to my daughter and my sister, the impact is still going on and this is what I want to stop. Does it ever stop, I asked myself? I don't know, but I do know that I want to find out how to make it better and help both my daughter and my sister. Bria and I talked some more and realized that we would need to talk about this again and again before we could really grasp all that had occurred and what lied ahead. What do I do next? I prayed to God for the answer. I knew what the answer was, so I continued to pray that God would give me the strength and guidance to take that next step - talking to my sister and my nieces. I prayed that I could handle the depth of the water we were treading through. With every day and every conversation, the water seemed to get deeper and deeper. I felt there was still more to uncover and the water was still rising.

Chapter 4

Wading Through Rising Water

After talking to Bria, I called my older sister. Her daughter answered the phone and said her mother wasn't home, but she would be back some time the next afternoon. So, I thought - what do I do now? I asked her if she had a few minutes to talk. She said she did and I took a deep gulp and began to tell her what I had discovered about Bria. I told her I had just found out she had been sexually molested as a child. Again, even though it pains me every time I say it - I revealed that it was my brother. She listened for a few minutes then told me that I should believe her. Here it is - more familiarity with the situation. She then began to tell me about her incident when my brother tried to molest *her* and she had fought him off. I quickly told her that I had no doubt that my daughter was telling the truth. I listened intently to her story. Not only did I want to hear what she had to say, but it was giving me time to digest this information yet again and also to collect my thoughts. I had not intended to have this conversation with her, so I felt like I needed to regroup and recollect my thoughts.

After listening to her story, I continued telling her the journey I had taken since discovering this information. After revealing more of my story, I began to share how I felt. I felt the urge more and more to want to kill my brother and I made no attempt to withhold my feelings. The anger in me continued to well up every time I thought about it - let alone talked about it. I told her that I would take this to the limit if I had to. I would get to the bottom of this and stop the hurt in **this** family. She told me that whatever my daughter and I wanted to do, she would support us - including prosecution. She also offered to talk to Bria and tell her own story. I assured her that I also was willing to do whatever my daughter wanted. I would support her 100%. This was for my daughter's healing as well as mine.

I told my niece I wanted to talk to her mother, but she said she needed to talk to her first - to prepare her. She knew that she was not going to take this well, so the preparation was necessary. I must say that I was feeling a bit confused because I knew that my sister had already been told about our younger sister, as well as her daughter. I tried to go with the flow, but I couldn't help but wonder why my niece needed to prepare her mother for something that she already knew. I decided to put that aside for the moment. I asked her to call me the next day when her mother returned home and she agreed. We ended our conversation, but I must say that the confusion was still lingering in my head. It had been a long day - I was tired, yet wired and angry, yet relieved in a sense. My emotions were still all over the place. I am usually pretty good at handling emotions, but this was a challenge which encompassed the magnitude of nothing I had ever seen before. I laid back and let my mind and body drift into a semi-sleep. I still had work to do and a plan to continue to map out.

I'm not sure how much sleep I got that night. I got up and went through my normal Sunday routine. I returned home from church and was preparing myself for what the rest of the day would bring. I knew what was ahead, but I didn't know how it was going to play out. By now, it was mid-afternoon and no one had called. By 4:00, my daughters were on the way over and I was anticipating a meeting with my sister and her daughter. Since I had not gotten a call yet from my sister or her daughter, I called them. My niece said that my sister was still not home yet, but she was expected by 5:00 p.m. I told her that Bria was coming over and I wanted them to be there as well so we could all talk. She said that since she still needed to talk to her mother, she suggested that we come over to their house later. My mind was telling me to decline the offer, so I asked her to call me after they talked. I really wanted to be in the comfort of my own home.

About two hours later my sister called. She immediately began saying how livid she was with our brother and how she couldn't understand how he would do such a thing. She told me she couldn't believe he abused my daughter. I chimed in with my thoughts and feelings and we had general conversation about the situation. I was a bit hesitant, because I was confused that she seemed unaware of any of the abuse. Maybe she didn't know about my daughter, but she certainly knew about our younger sister.

I began to talk about why our brother would do such a thing. I talked about how a large percentage of abusers have also been abused themselves. I told my sister how I had wondered over the years whenever I would hear about the abuse in the Catholic Church, whether our brother could have been one of their victims. We went to Catholic school growing up and there was certainly opportunity. I recalled that the 'privileged' or 'chosen' students were asked to come to the convent (where the nuns lived) and the rectory (where the priests lived). This was a big deal to be chosen to do this and I recall having had this opportunity many times. I am certain my brother did as well. Students who were chosen to go to the convent or rectory, helped the priests and nuns with various chores. I remember going to the convent to help sort the candy orders that came in. Each classroom got part of the shipment and they needed to be sorted before being delivered to each room. This was a big deal to those of us who were chosen and I certainly enjoyed it. I am not certain what jobs the boys who helped the priests were assigned. I'm in no way saying that abuse was going on in our parish, but I have to admit that I often wondered if my brother had been exposed to it.

My sister and I continued our conversation and I was still waiting to hear her say she was coming over. I decided to go somewhere I didn't want to go, as we continued to figure out what happened over the years. I told her that I believed there was no way that our father could have done anything to our brother. My sister quickly said that she also felt there was no way that happened. I was relieved that she agreed with me. Nothing in life is impossible - as we have surely learned, but that would be the closest thing to an impossibility for me.

After a few more minutes passed, I looked out the window and saw a car pull into the driveway. I noticed that it was my oldest niece's car. I saw her and my middle niece get out. I continued talking to my sister as they came into the house. I decided to continue talking before I went downstairs. I talked again about what could make our brother do these things. At that point, my sister said something that caused me to hold my breath. She said that *'she hoped that she didn't do anything to make our brother act in the way he had'*. I thought to myself, what a strange thing to say. I imagine my silence prompted her to continue talking. She said there was one thing that she remembered happening when we were growing up and she hopes that this didn't cause him to do such things. She told me that one time our brother came to her and showed her his penis. He said, "Look what I have." They laughed and that was the end of it. She didn't think anything of it then and even now, quickly dismissed it as something kids do when they discover they are different. Even so, this seemed strange to me. The strange part was that she had admitted it. I would have never guessed she would tell me something like that. It made me wonder what else she wasn't saying. I decided not to explore it any further at that moment.

After several more minutes, I heard the sounds of crying coming from downstairs. I assumed the girls were talking, so I decided to let them have their time together before I joined them. After about ten minutes, my husband came up to our bedroom and asked if I was coming down to join the conversation and I said yes. I told my sister that her daughters were at my house and I needed to talk with them. I expected her to say that she would be over. She didn't. Instead, she said she would talk to me later (*What??*). I didn't ask, but hung up and went downstairs.

My daughters and my nieces were sitting in the living room talking. I pulled up a chair to be closer to them and listened. I saw their tears; I heard them talking. As I sat there listening; digging for explanations concerning how and why such a tragedy could occur in our own family, I suddenly got that sinking feeling again. I thought *this can't be*! The more I listened it became clear that there had been another casualty - my oldest niece. Life and time stood still for me again at the very moment I realized this cycle of dysfunction was expanding. So here was the gap I had feared; my brother had abused my younger sister and also tried to abuse my middle niece. I wondered what, if anything he had done in between. I now had my answer - another casualty in the family.

My oldest niece was talking and once I realized she was speaking about her abuse, I asked for confirmation. She said that my brother had also abused her, not tried - but had succeeded. I burst into tears again from the pain. This is too much to bear. She didn't go into much detail and I didn't want to press for more. I remember her saying that she couldn't believe she allowed him to coax her with cookies to do things. I assured her that as a child, she had no way of knowing right from wrong - or that it wasn't supposed to be happening to her. I soon realized that her mother did not know about this until right before my nieces came to my house. It was beginning to come together for me; this was why my niece was insistent about talking to her mother before I talked to her. My niece knew that her older sister needed to talk to her mother and reveal her abuse. She needed to hear it from her and not me. I didn't know what to say, think, or feel. I was as numb as I would be if I had been given anesthesia. I asked a few questions, but mostly I just sat and listened.

The girls talked some more and I continued to listen. My nieces told me they had talked to their younger sister and she confirmed that my brother had not abused her. I was relieved to hear that. When she and my younger daughter were growing up, my mother had remarried and my brother didn't spend much time at her house. The girls talked about how they were relieved that this secret was finally out. Even though they anticipated that it would not make the pain go away completely, at least they didn't have to carry around the secret any longer - it was out. They pledged to support each other. Even if they moved forward with seeking prosecution, they would all be in agreement and support the decision. Everyone agreed there was more to do, but at least this was the beginning of the road to healing.

When my nieces left, my daughters and I talked a bit more but mostly we sat in stunned disbelief. My daughters left to go home for the night and I was still numb. My brain hurt, I needed to lie down and rest - but I still had things to figure out, so sleep probably would not come easily. I was still slightly confused; did I correctly hear my younger sister say she had talked to my older sister 20 years ago when she remembered her own abuse? I decide to call my younger sister to verify and she confirmed that she *did* talk to her. In fact, that's how my younger sister knew about the attempt on my middle niece. I couldn't figure out why my sister didn't share this with me, but I decided it wasn't an issue at the top of my list at that moment. I would revisit it later.

Chapter 5

Painful Decisions

The next day passed and my feelings and emotions were still all over the place. I talked with my younger sister again and we explored our options regarding prosecuting our brother. We discovered that the law is not clear and somewhat convoluted to understand. If we were reading it correctly, we believed that the only person who still fell within the statute of limitations was my daughter Bria. My sister made calls to the Crime Victims Unit and to an attorney in our hometown, to get clarity on the laws regarding the statute of limitation on reporting and prosecuting child sexual abuse. We wanted to be prepared just in case we needed to take that road. If we did - and the law is as we understood it, this would be a heavy burden for Bria to carry. I began to see why she was concerned about what this would do to the family. The reality was that she could be blamed for causing an already-festering wound to get even bigger. The attorney promised to get back to my sister by the end of that day or early the next morning. All we could do was wait.

A few days after my daughters and nieces met at my house, I called my mother to let her know that my daughter and I wanted to talk to her. My daughter said she was uncertain about taking any action in this matter, because she didn't want to cause any more unrest in the family. She did not want to be the cause of my nieces or anyone else not talking to my mother. This came about because many of the conversations that had taken place so far - all included feelings from everyone that my mother had known about my brother's predator nature for a long time and she did nothing to protect the children from him.

When I talked to my mother that morning she updated me that she was planning to see my brother that day. As she said, "I want him to tell me face-to-face." *Hmm, does she not believe us?* I felt like elaborating on this comment, but I was getting ready for work and decided I didn't want to spend time on this at that moment - especially if it was going to cause me to get frustrated. I told her that my daughter and I would be over to talk with her on Thursday evening, which was two days away. She again said that she planned to talk to my brother by then. I hoped she did and that the conversation would bring out the truth in him. I also hoped that the conversation would give our mother another opportunity to accept and acknowledge who and what he is.

On Thursday morning I called my mother to remind her that my daughter and I would be over to see her that evening. She stated she had gone to see my brother. I held my breath waiting to hear what I feared - however, I heard the opposite. She said that he had admitted abusing my daughter. I was almost speechless - but quickly acknowledged that I heard what she said. Reality was surfacing again. I asked her to tell me everything he said and she stated that she would talk to us when we got there that evening. I followed up with asking her if there was anything that she should tell me *before* we got there. I was concerned he had said something that maybe Bria shouldn't hear. I wanted to try to filter out any information that could cause unnecessary trauma. My main concern was my brother possibly blaming Bria for causing the abuse to happen. I was in 'protective mother mode'. Since my mother would not divulge any information yet, I decided I would prep Bria before we got there.

Another long ride to my mother's house created an atmosphere of anticipation and angst. I told Bria that my mother had talked to my brother and he admitted abusing her, but I didn't have any other information yet. It was hard for me to tell her that, but I wanted to prepare her before she heard it from my mother. Bria and I talked about what we thought we would hear when we got there and where it would all lead. What would happen if we took the road to prosecution? Again - the 'what ifs'? The ride did not seem as long as it had days ago. I welcomed the fact that I was not making the trip alone. We arrived at my mother's house and again without much chatter, we got right to the matter at hand. I asked my mother what my brother had to say. I quickly got the sense that her conversation was going to be cryptic. She began to tell us about my brother's admission. She said that in addition to admitting that he abused my nieces and my daughter - he confessed that *he* had also been abused. I fully expected (if he was even to be believed) this was going to lead to the revelation of abuse while he was attending Catholic school, but to my astonishment, it didn't.

My mother continued to tell the story. She said that she didn't ask who had abused him. She didn't want to know. I sat there thinking - *how could you **not** want to know who abused your child*? My mind was racing again, but in the midst of all that was being said - or not said, I realized that my mother was saying 'she' (*she*)? Does this mean my brother was abused by a female? My mother was still talking, but at that point I was not really hearing what she was saying. I was still stuck on her not wanting to know who abused her son. I cut her off and asked her why she didn't want to know; she stumbled over her words and said she just didn't want to. This was not making sense to me. I snapped back at her and said that whether or not she wanted to know, *I wanted to know*. I asked her who 'she' was. My mother still said that she didn't know, but I told her I thought she did. I told her she could deny it, but I suspected I knew who 'she' was. I told her that the person I was referring to had already somewhat admitted it to me. I asked her if 'she' was my older sister. She reluctantly admitted that it was. *Boom!* Another bomb has hit. I knew there was more to my older sister wondering if she had done anything to cause our brother's inappropriate behavior and her revelation of his exposing himself to her. My mother admitted she didn't want to reveal this for fear of causing more problems. I told her that I intended to talk to my sister. I looked at my daughter and she seemed to be in a trance. I'm sure she didn't know what to think or say. So now, not just my brother has abused - but my sister too! What is next? I didn't want to think about it, but I had to. I needed to continue moving forward, although I was dreading what was around the next corner.

We sat in utter silence for what seemed like an eternity, but in reality it was really just a few minutes. There wasn't much more to say, so I got up to leave. My daughter followed my lead and we said our goodbyes. Here again was another long, slow walk down the hall to the elevator. The only difference was that this time, I was not walking alone - but the numbness was still the same. During the ride home, my daughter and I talked about what had just happened. We were both struggling for the right words to say. We were in utter disbelief about the revelation concerning my sister's role in this cycle of abuse. After more talking, we both came to the conclusion that this revelation had changed the landscape of the ordeal. We both acknowledged that my brother - although what he had done was monstrous, is himself a victim. This painted the picture a little differently, in that there was another rung on the ladder to climb before we could get to the top and begin to find our way back to the bottom.

I realized that my conversation with my sister now had to change direction from ally, to accused. It was much easier to acknowledge my brother as having done something horrendous, but I must admit it was much more difficult to accept that my sister had done something horrific. I think it is because of the closer relationship that I've had with my sister, even though a distance had existed in recent years. Never the less, no matter how difficult it would be, I knew I needed to confront her as well. I had to keep focus on the fact that my daughter had been hurt and this entire story must be uncovered if she has a fair chance of beginning her healing.

Amazingly, the ride home didn't seem so long. With each facet of this dilemma that was uncovered, there came a pang of relief that another step had been taken and was behind us. By this time, I had accepted that I must prepare myself for anything that might be revealed; no matter how painful and disturbing it might be. I must work through the pain if I wanted to reach a point of healing. We got back to my house, said our goodbyes and my daughter drove home. I closed the door, stood there and let out a sigh that I'd been holding in for the last 2 hours. What just happened? Is this just a dream?

The next morning I called my mother and told her I wanted to talk to my brother. I asked her to call him and let him know that I didn't want to have a confrontation with him, I just needed to talk. She agreed to call and tell him. I told her I would talk to her when I got home that evening. I mustered up the strength to finish getting dressed and go to work. I hoped the day would go by fast. I anticipated having 2 more critical conversations - one with my brother and the other with my older sister. I did not look forward to the latter. To get through the day, I tried hard to put the nightmare out of my mind - if only for the next 8 hours. I prayed, *God, please give me strength!*

I returned home, went upstairs and lay on the bed for a few minutes. I knew what I needed to do. I had to call my brother. I called my mother first to see if she had talked to him. She said that she had and he told her he would welcome the chance to talk to me and my daughter. I was surprised and glad to hear it at the same time. As fate would have it, she then revealed his remaining comments. He would talk to us - but not now. "Oh no!" I immediately shouted. "He has had over 40 years to be silent; he is not going to get away with that now. He's going to talk to me!" I told my mother I was calling him right then; I called, but he didn't answer.

I called my mother back and told her to call him; thinking that he would answer her call. She called me back, saying that she had talked to him. He would come to her house the next day and he would call me using her phone, because he has limited minutes on his. I told her that if he was coming to her house, then I would much rather talk to him in person and would come there. She called me back and said he was okay with me coming to talk with him, but he didn't want to be met with a roomful of people ready to pounce on him. I assured my mother I would come by myself and would not tell anyone about the meeting - except my husband. I was sure he would want to come and support me. I let my mother know that my brother and I could go into another room to talk in private. Another long night ahead!

I woke the next morning with very little sleep. The clock ticked by very slowly. I wished it would quickly get to 12:00 - the time of my meeting with my brother. My husband and I drove to my mother's house and the ride was quiet. He asked me a couple of times if I was okay and I assured him that I was. He quietly drove and I looked out the window as if I had never seen the sites before. If you asked me what I was looking at, I couldn't tell you. Although I have seen those sites a million times; it was all such a blur. Finally, we got to the house and I rang the buzzer to let my mother know we were there. I said my hellos to the doormen and got on the elevator for the all-too familiar ride up. I was feeling reluctant, but anxious. No time to slow down now. I saw my mother standing at the door. Ready or not...

Chapter 6

Facing My Fears

I haven't seen my brother in more than 10 years. The last time I saw him, I didn't recognize him at first. He looked so different than he had before. If my mother had not been with me, I would have walked right past him. This time, I didn't know what to expect. No matter what the circumstances, I didn't want to see him in bad shape. I knew he had been sick over the years and thought that he would be showing the effects of his illness. I imagined how he would look, but to my surprise he looked much better than he had more than 10 years ago. I felt a sigh of relief. I walked over to him and spoke. The circumstances of this visit prevented me from reaching out and giving him a hug. One side of my brain told me to reach out to him, but my heart and soul reminded me of why I was there - he abused my child! This fact overwhelmed any thought of showing him any sign of affection. I immediately asked if he wanted to go in the other room to talk. He said he would rather sit in the dining room, because the chair was better for his back. I told him my husband would move the chairs to the other room - I preferred to talk in private. He agreed and we went into the room.

As the chairs were being moved, I prayed that I would be able to keep my composure and remain calm. I wanted to make the best of this conversation. I knew it might be my only chance to say what I had to say to him. I did not want to live with 'what ifs' because I had forgotten something I wanted to say - or my words didn't come out the way I wanted them to. I trusted God to hear me and guide my thoughts and words. Once the chairs were in the room, I asked if we could have prayer. My husband, mother and I reached out to hold hands and we reached for my brother's hand. He refused, saying that he did not know what God we served, so he would not participate in any act of prayer. Wow, I hadn't expected this. I reached for my mother's hand and asked my husband to pray. As I tried hard to focus on the prayer (God knows we needed it), I was comforted with this thought - my brother may not want to participate in the prayer, but he would surely hear it. That was good enough for me.

I sat down and began to tell my brother why I needed to talk to him (as if he didn't know). I let him know that I didn't intend for this conversation to be confrontational. I thanked him for agreeing to talk to me. So, enough with the preliminaries; it was time to get on with the unpleasant task. It was important for me to keep eye contact with him. I wanted him to look at me when I was talking. I didn't want to make this conversation with him easy. He didn't make it easy for my daughter when he chose to abuse her, so I didn't want to let him off easy by not having to look at the pain on my face. I began to tell him how he has hurt my daughter and me. I told him how much it has hurt me as a mother to not know why my daughter's behavior over the years has been problematic at times. I told him how painful it was to not know why. Despite all the love, guidance and opportunity that Bria has had, she often chose to make very bad decisions. I told him that with the revelation of his abuse, I now have some answers. Even with this revelation, I can't pretend that I know what to do now to help her. I prayed that God will guide us through.

I had many questions I wanted to ask him, but I wanted to do it in such a way that would keep him talking and not clam up. It was important for me to release this so I could move on, and more importantly - help my daughter get through this ordeal. To my surprise, he willingly participated in the conversation. He said that he took full responsibility for what he had done. He said that he was sorry it happened. I sat there stunned that he had admitted this without me having to pry it out of him. I wanted him to continue to be talk openly, so I tried hard to listen more than I talked. Tears were welling up in me again, but I tried hard to control them because I wanted to remain focused to make the best out of the conversation. I was thinking that this conversation would be the last piece of the puzzle - or would it?

My brother confirmed what my daughter had already told me. Nothing really new was revealed, so this made me feel better. I don't know what I would have done if he added more details that would magnify the hurt more. I told him that I knew about him abusing our younger sister. My brother's conversation moved to another level of detail - *why* this had happened. He told me that he didn't know how much I knew about sexual abuse, but that most abusers have been abused. I assured him I was familiar with that fact. He began to tell me that he himself was abused. He confirmed what our mother already told me; he tells me that he was abused by our older sister.

The abuse took place from the time he was about 3 years old until he was about 7 or 8. He remembers maybe being in school for about 2 years when his abuse stopped. He said that when the abuse stopped, he didn't know what to do. From a child's mind and perspective, he asked himself why she stopped *playing* with him in such a way. Why would she not want to do this anymore; especially without giving him an explanation? I asked him if he talked to her about it and he said he had not. He was just left to wonder on his own. He eventually came to the conclusion that this is what was supposed to happen and that he now was supposed to do what was done to him. So, this is why he began abusing our younger sister! Through my tears, I asked him why he chose her. I asked him if he had ever done anything to me and he said he did not. He said that since he and I are one year apart in age, I was too close to him. Based on what he had learned, he thought he should do this with someone younger than he. After all, there were 6 years between him and our older sister, so - left to figure it out on his own, this was the logical way for him to think.

He continued on to say that one of the horrible aspects of sexual abuse is that sex generally feels good. There are some instances where it is painful, but often the physical act feels good - which causes all types of confusion in the minds of victims. After several years of his abuse, he had developed a dependency on these interactions, so this contributed to his confusion and lack of understanding when it ended. He continued to talk about how he felt being abused. Even though he was so young, he thought it may be wrong because it was something that was done in private and that was kept secret from our parents. This led to me asking if he told our parents when it stopped. He responded that he had not.

We talked further and he shared how he felt a normal life had been taken from him because of the abuse he suffered. He acknowledged that he in no way was using his abuse as an excuse or justification of his abuse of others; although he does think that it is a big contributing factor. The fork in the road came when he was old enough to make the choice to stop abusing others. Although this may seem like a logical thing to do, it almost never happens without help. He continued to talk about never wanting to get married because he felt that he would have those same abusive tendencies with his children and he did not want to do that. I wish he had had that same level of restraint and discipline with other children. I can't help but think of the loss of innocence that would have been spared if he had made the same choice of restraint with them.

I didn't know what to think or how to feel as I sat there in the moment. I continued to ask questions and he continued to answer them - I believe with honesty. This helped me to gain a sense of calm which helped the mood of the conversation. He talked about how he felt like he was our sister's own sexual experiment; explaining how he was told what to do and how. I asked if he had ever gotten help with his problem and he said that he had done so about 12 years ago. He had experienced two losses in his life; his girlfriend, who was about 25 years older than him and then the loss of their dog that they had for many years. These events put him in a state of depression that led him to know he needed professional help if he was to maintain any degree of sanity. He also knew that his history of abuse - both being abused and being an abuser, still had a major impact on his life.

What he told me next shook me in such a way that had I not been sitting down, I would have fallen to my knees. He told me that he had gone to our mother for help when he was about 20 years old. Before I could grasp what he said, he went on to say how she had chosen to 'sweep it under the rug'; not just on that occasion, but on subsequent occasions over the years when he would talk to her. It made sense to me now how she had chosen to pretty much ignore my sister when she told her about her abuse. Could our mother be in denial about all of this? Could her way of handling this, be to totally ignore it and hope that it would go away? Did she think that if she ignored it, it didn't exist? Whatever the case, I was shocked that she knew this all these years. This also meant that when he was abusing my nieces and daughter, our mother knew about his problem.

The anger was building up in me as I realized that she knew she needed to protect our daughters from him and she chose not to do so. Whether this was intentional or not, she failed to keep them safe. My mind was racing in many different directions yet again. I wanted to keep focused on my conversation with my brother, but I couldn't help but wonder why our mother had ignored this issue. I knew she was in the next room and I could easily call her in the room with us. As if he was reading my mind, my brother said we could call her in the room if I wanted to verify what he was saying. I told him no - I believed him, so there was no need. I would talk to her later. Today, I do regret that we didn't call her in the room. In hindsight, it may have eliminated the denial that would continue as the days and weeks passed.

We continued to talk. My brother asked if I would tell our older sister that he didn't feel any animosity towards her for what she had done to him. However, he wanted to know if she ever thought about how what she did to him, may have affected his life. He knew I planned to talk to her about his revelations to me, so I told him I would relay his message. After an exhausting couple of hours, I felt the need to bring the conversation to a close. I believed I had all I needed for the time being. I told my brother that when I came to talk to him, I had every intention of pursuing prosecution, if the law allowed. After hearing the story of his abuse, I was not so sure it was the best thing to do. I told him that I could not speak for my daughter, but I was pretty sure she would feel the same way. He thanked me and said he appreciated not having to spend his remaining life in prison. He told me that his health is very poor and his heart is failing. Although he did not want to go to prison - he was willing to accept that, if it was to be his fate. He believed that he deserved to be punished for what he had done and he had been cautiously waiting for the knock on his door ever since he found out that I was pursuing this matter. Even after all that had taken place and how enraged I was feeling, I still could not bear to inflict intentional pain on him by having him worry about when that knock would come. After all, I must acknowledge that he is a victim too. On that note, I got up and our conversation ended.

I walked into the room where my husband and mother were sitting. I walked over to get my bag and told my husband that I was ready to leave. My brother said his goodbyes and he left. My mother sat down and asked what happened. I had no desire to talk to her right then. I told her I was leaving and would talk to her later. Here we go again - another long walk down the hallway. This is becoming all too familiar and painful. On the ride home, I updated my husband on what happened. He was as stunned as I was to hear about my brother's honesty and willingness to talk. As he drove, he tried his best to comfort me without being able to reach out and put his arms around me. Even still, I felt the warmth of his intent and it felt good. I knew I still had a long way to go on this journey and his support would be critical to my sanity. God knows what we need and when we need it. I thank Him for his faithfulness. I needed that reassurance right then because I had another difficult road ahead to travel - another talk with my older sister

Chapter 7

Putting All the Pieces Together

Reluctantly, I knew I needed to talk to my older sister again. I just talked with my brother the day before, so I was fresh on the heels of that conversation and still had not processed it all. My mind told me I needed to get this next conversation over with as soon as possible because I believed this was the last piece of the puzzle - or so I hoped. I didn't think I could stand one more bit of information that I was not aware of. I knew I couldn't move forward with a solution until I talked to everyone I thought was involved and I had as much information as possible. I just wanted this to be over, but I knew it was far from that.

My sister and I met. I wanted to meet at a neutral place so that neither of us felt at a disadvantage or uncomfortable with our surroundings. I love sitting by the water so I suggested we go sit and talk at a local park where the water is a soothing backdrop. However, it was a steaming hot day, so sitting out in the sun didn't really seem like an appealing idea. We decided to meet at my house. I quickly asked my husband if he would get lost for a couple of hours so we could have privacy. Being the amazing and accommodating person that he is, without hesitation he quickly left; wishing me well as he went out the door. I wanted him to go, but I wanted him to stay. I needed that shoulder to lean on at the moment, but knew I had to walk this alone. My anticipation was high as I waited for my sister. My mind was racing as I thought about whether I should have waited a while before we had this next meeting. I was sure she was at a loss as to why we were talking about this again. But, then I wondered - does she really know? The doorbell rang and the thump in my heart let me know that the next step was in motion and there was no turning back. I had to pull myself together and get ready.

We sat down and if I remember correctly, we didn't spend much time on idle 'how-do-you-dos'. I told her I met with our brother and there were some things I needed to talk to her about as a result of that conversation. I saw the look on her face. It was a look of concern, but not of surprise. This actually provided me a bit of comfort to think I was not over-reaching by digging deeper into this nightmare. I knew it was important that I didn't cause her to shut down or become defensive; however, I also knew that I needed to let her know facts quickly so that she couldn't evade the reality of what I knew had taken place. As I began telling her about my meeting with our brother, I told her that he acknowledged he told our mother about his problem years ago. She quickly focused on our mother and the role she played over the years in 'protecting' our brother. I knew I didn't want to go down that road because I now know that a lot of her feelings regarding how our mother handled our brother are misplaced. At the least - they are understandable, given what we now know occurred.

In rapid succession, I let my sister know that our brother admitted to abusing my daughter. He admitted he was wrong and that he wishes it had never happened. I informed her that he told me he is ready for whatever penalty he had to pay - even if it meant going to prison. I shared with her that he asked me if I knew much about the cycle of abuse; then he revealed that he himself had been a victim of sexual abuse. Upon hearing this, my sister responded by saying that she was not surprised he would offer an excuse for his actions. I told her about the cycle of sexual abuse and the fact that most abusers have themselves been abused. I knew I needed to go into further detail to temper her feedback. I began to tell her the details of our brother's story about being abused by her. She was not at all surprised.

A significant part of my brother's story for me was him saying that he came to know that abuse was wrong – however as an 8-year-old, he was doing what he was 'taught' to do. Once his abuse from her ended, he was left with the dilemma of what to do next. His feelings - both physical and emotional, didn't stop; so he eventually did what he thought he was supposed to do – 'do to someone else what was done to him'. This wasn't in a vengeful way, but simply as a matter of logic for a child who was forced into a world of thoughts and feelings he was ill-equipped to handle - simply from lack of maturity, wisdom and development. Children do what they learn and that's what he did. I had to at least acknowledge that.

As I continued to reveal the events of the previous day, I saw the retreat in her demeanor. After revealing more and more of what our brother told me, my sister expressed remorse for what she had done and the impact it has had on her children and my daughter. I saw the need to switch gears and take on the role of consoler. I let her know that whatever happened between her and our brother was in the past - as all of this was and there is nothing that we can do to change what has happened. We can only move forward. I told her our brother sent her a message that he does not hold any animosity towards her, but that he does wonder if she ever thinks about how she has affected his life. I told her that I love her. She said she didn't believe it because she doesn't understand how anyone could love her after knowing what she did. I assured her that I do.

This dialogue about love was a surprise to me. I did not anticipate having this conversation, so I quickly regrouped and gave her what she needed at the moment - compassion. I felt sympathy for her; this couldn't be easy for her to admit that she had played a major role in this horrible nightmare. The realization that it began with her is not easy for me to accept. She said that she didn't know how she could face our children. I assured her that she could. She needed time, but she could do it and I would be there to help her. I knew going into this conversation that I would need to extend the same compassion to her that I had extended to our brother. I had to put a lot of things that happened between us over the years aside; the things that have caused our relationship to lose its closeness. It's not about who was right or wrong - who did what and why or what's fair or unfair. None of that stuff in the past matters much now. It's about moving forward - forgiving and surviving. I didn't think she felt the same right at that moment, but I'm sure eventually she will be able to rationalize this and come to terms with her guilt, pain, or whatever else she is feeling.

After a bit more discussion, she gathered her things and said she needed to go. We stood up; I attempted to hug her and tell her again that I love her, but I got the same response as previously. She blocked my embrace, so I decided to back off and give her space. I told her that I would be there for her - whatever and whenever she needed me. After she left, I felt empty and unsure of this being the beginning of the healing process. I realized that another layer of complexity had been added to the saga and I didn't know where to go from there. I knew that now wasn't the time to discuss this, but I couldn't help wondering where this all began with her – if, who, what, when. As much as I wanted this to be the end, I asked myself the seemingly-selfish question; *now where do I begin?*

Chapter 8

Where Do I Begin?

No one expects their family can be prey to such an unthinkable tragedy. I surely didn't. Not that I think we are better than the next family or impenetrable, but never something like this. The discovery of child sexual abuse in our family is no longer a long-silent secret between us. The layers of the abuse have been peeled back and the silent screams can now be heard. My emotions are still all over the place. Anger, hurt, frustration, sense of relief, confusion, concern… I could go down every letter of the alphabet and come up with an applicable emotion right now. Angry, broken, confused, distraught - all are appropriate feelings of having been through the nightmare of discovering this horrible silent secret that has crippled lives and relationships in our family for decades. Some have been living with knowing and holding this secret; some living through it in complete cluelessness. The healing must and can now begin, but how do we go on? Where do we start? I need to admit - I feel helpless and I don't really know what comes next. There are still layers that need to be peeled back to get through the process of healing. This is only the beginning. I am not naive enough to think that this will be easy, but one thing we have in our favor is that there is an overwhelming sense of relief that this is out in the open.

I am quickly realizing that I have a heavy burden to carry. In the months since this ordeal began, there was little time to think about the aftermath. Now, since I have stepped back and taken a breath - I realize that everyone is probably experiencing their own hell. I think about what that might mean. How will they really feel about the release of this secret? How will they feel about me bringing it out into the open? How will they feel about our mother, our brother and my older sister who is the mother of two of his victims?

In the quickness with which this has all been revealed, we didn't have much time to experience the typical feelings that are often felt when sexual abuse in a family is discovered. These feelings include shock, rage, confusion, denial, disbelief and guilt. In processing this, I decided that I needed to prepare myself for anything. To deal with these possible reactions in the aftermath would require time, strength and support from each other, friends - extended family and maybe even professionals in support service areas, such as counseling. We all may deal with this in different ways. Some will choose to move on without needing help. Some may choose counseling or other ways to help them understand how to move on. Some of us may lean on each other for support; others may choose to go it alone or seek help outside of the family. Some may need help and not even recognize it. Whichever way we choose, it will be important that we are able to move forward with a minimum of further dysfunction.

I recognize that I won't be able to solve everything, although I feel a sense of responsibility for having brought this all to the surface. I do need to begin with what I can do. What I realize that I can and must do - is heal myself from my brokenness of this discovery. So, the question for me becomes - where do I begin? How do I deal with the emotions – the, hurt, pain, anger, guilt and uncertainty? So, I have to start with where I am right now. I need to first forgive my mother. Facing the reality that sexual abuse has occurred in our family is painful. Knowing my mother - whom I have trusted and held in high regard all my life, has played a major role in this secrecy, is unthinkable. Life tells us that we shouldn't hold anyone on too high a pedestal, but your mother can be a person whom you think is exempt from that adage. My reasoning mind tells me that I need to find a way to move past what I feel and find a place where my heart can be at rest. Right now, it is feeling broken. I pray that the break heals soon.

Forgiveness is a must - no exceptions. I must put the pieces in place. I admit I can understand why my mother may have chosen to not tell our father what happened. I can even understand why she may not have wanted anyone to find out. I'm sure she didn't want people to know that our family was not the 'almost perfect' family it appeared to be. I'm sure she didn't want to bear the talk that was sure to occur. I get all this. What I can't seem to come to grips with is why she didn't do everything in her power to keep our children away from our brother. I can think of all kinds of ways she could have done this without letting a soul know what he had done, or was capable of doing. This I can't understand. Right now, it feels like I may never be able to understand it, even though I know I can't stay in the place I am now.

Some months passed and I found myself still in the same place. I knew I couldn't ignore this much longer. I had to face things and get to a better place. I struggled over the previous months with my relationship and communication with my mother. We have always been close, but lately I had a hard time having a conversation with her past the level of idle chit chat. I would call to check up on her and see how she was doing, but beyond that, I struggled with what to say. One morning I called her for my usual check-up call. I quickly detected an attitude in her voice. I asked her what was wrong and she snapped back that she was fine. This was very much out of her character, so I moved on to the next conversation only to be met with a similar response. I again asked what was wrong; receiving the same result. I didn't let it slide that time. I pressed her for a true response about what was wrong. She finally said that it seemed no one wanted to talk to her. I told her that I was dealing with a lot at the moment, so if it seemed that I didn't want to talk to her - the truth was that I didn't quite know what to say. I explained to her that I was dealing with a lot of the fall-out from the revelation of the abuse in our family. My daughter and I were in a cooling-off period where we needed some time apart. As I had expected, she blamed me for what my brother did to her. I know that she doesn't really feel that way in her heart - but I did anticipate that when it would be an easy jab at me for her to use, she would use it. I told my mother this was a huge matter and that we all needed time to deal with it in our own way. I told her that I may not have handled it the way that she chose, but it was imperative that the secret was not kept quiet any longer. I asked her if she was mad at me - and even though she said no, I heard in her voice that she felt otherwise. I knew I was at the moment of decision. I must move past this point. Back to the question - *where do I begin?*

A couple days later, I decided that I had to go and visit my mother and tell her face-to-face how I was really feeling. I had realized that I couldn't get past where I was until I had an honest conversation with her about what all this had done to me and how I was feeling about her role in it. Over the next day, I tussled back and forth about what I would say. I knew the key issue for me, was how I was feeling about her not protecting our children by keeping them away from our brother. Another issue was that she was continuously denying that she had any knowledge of our brother's problems. I believed my younger sister when she said that she confronted our mother over 20 years ago. I believed my brother when he said that he had first gone to our mother for help when he was about 20 years old. However, she continued to deny to all of us that she knew anything. These two things were nagging at me and preventing me from relating to her as I had in the past. There was a part of me that wanted to just get over it, but another part of me wanted to confront her and let her know that these things were bothering me. I struggled with what to do, until now. I felt I would never be able to have the same kind of relationship with her until this was resolved. I knew I had to go see her again. After all, it was now time to think about me and that is what I intended to do - what's best for me. Getting this out was best for me and what I needed to help me heal. Funny how the best-laid plans often don't go as we think they will. As I would soon find out, this was certainly one of those times.

Another long drive alone to my mother's house proved to be another trip of replaying a scripted conversation over and over in my mind. I arrived and she greeted me with a hug at the door. As I walked into her home and sat down, I made a decision that I would shape my discussion based on how our conversation was going. It didn't take long for me to decide that it was no longer necessary for me to confront my mother with what I thought were the issues that were holding me back. As I sat there looking into her eyes as we talked idle chit chat, I knew that despite whatever decisions she had made in the past; for whatever reasons, she was still the mother and grandmother that loved us unconditionally and with everything that she could. I knew that she would never knowingly sit back and let our children be abused. I believe that she thought she had it under control. At that moment, I felt true forgiveness and compassion. I felt for her and not for me. I imagined that this is how God must feel about us. He forgives unconditionally. As much as I thought I needed to think about me, I really needed to think about her. We talked as we watched a movie together. I had only planned to be there a short while - maybe 20 minutes, but it turned into a 2-1/2 hour visit. When I left, we walked down the hall to the elevator and I had a sense of peace that I had not felt in the visits there over the last few months since all this had taken place. We got down to the lobby and hugged goodbye with the old familiar warmth and strength. I realized that it wasn't about needing to confront her, but needing to forgive her. Not for her, but for me. I was at peace.

Epilogue.....

As this book concludes, this is not the ending to this story. I don't know that there will ever be an ending. I imagine that it will take many more months and maybe even years to get to a place where this will be a much less painful memory. As painful as this situation is, I believe that there is a reason why this happened and it will benefit somebody, somewhere along the way. Why we were chosen to go through this, I don't know. I don't understand it and I would never have signed up for it. But it happened and we have to move on from it. We need to forgive, to heal and to love.

I have made small steps to heal my family relationships. I've made a decision to forgive my mother and work to regain the closeness we have always had. I've reached out to my brother, but he hasn't responded to my call. My daughter and I still struggle with our 'good days, bad days' relationship. My younger sister still struggles with the scars of her abuse. My older sister and I have taken baby steps to strengthen our relationship, but we have a long way to go. At least the intent is there and for that I am grateful. I haven't discussed this with my nieces since the initial days of this discovery. I will, but it just hasn't happened yet. I've started therapy for myself and my husband will take part. We have pledged to not let anything rock our marriage off of its foundation.

Only time will tell how each of us will weather this storm. What I do know is that God is in control of everything. We must ask Him to give us new mercies each day. Guide, direct and protect us as we navigate this life. Ask Him to keep His arms outstretched around us to keep all danger from us. Bless those we come in contact with so they will not bring any harm to us. Forgiveness is hard work. Forgiving is essential to the healing process. As we release our hurts, we are then free to be healed and to grow beyond our pain.

The Lord is the strength of my life--of whom shall I be afraid?
Psalms 27:1

www.ingramcontent.com/pod-product-compliance
Lightning Source LLC
Chambersburg PA
CBHW060143050426
42448CB00010B/2263